Dedicated to my wife and son

Vamos a preguntarle!

Let's ask him!

¿Quieres saltar?

Do you want to hop?

No, no, no

¿Quieres Jugar?

Do you want to play?

Sí, sí, sí

Yes, yes, yes

¿Quieres caminar?

Do you want to walk?

No, no, no

¿Quieres Correr?

Do you want to run?

Si, si, si

Yes, yes, yes

¿Quieres comer?

Do you want to eat?

No, no, no

¿Quieres Agua?

Do you want water?

Sí, sí, sí

Yes, yes, yes

¿Quieres dormir?

Do you want to sleep?

No, no, no

¿Quieres bañarte?

Do you want to shower?

Sí, sí, sí

Yes, yes, yes

¿Quieres cantar?

Do you want to sing?

No, no, no

¿Quieres bailar?

Do you want to dance?

Sí, sí, sí

Yes, yes, yes

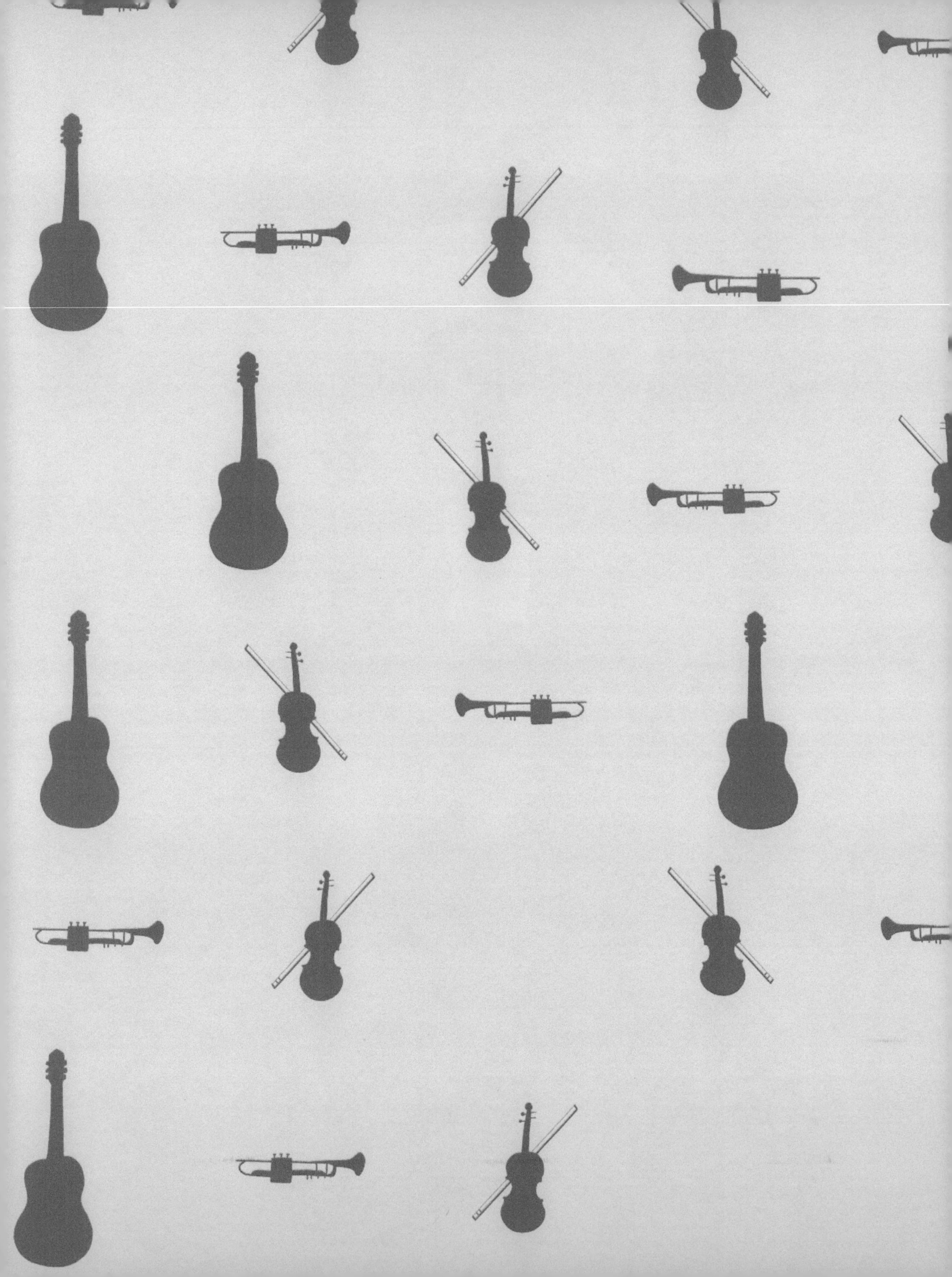

www.ingramcontent.com/pod-product-compliance
Ingram Content Group UK Ltd.
Pitfield, Milton Keynes, MK11 3LW, UK
UKHW060116300726
14090UKWH00002B/231

* 9 7 9 8 5 0 0 1 7 3 9 3 5 *